SHEPHERD ME, LORD

DAILY REFLECTIONS FOR YOUR LENTEN JOURNEY

DR. TOM CURRAN

EDITED BY TRISTAN BEACH

MCF PRESS

SHEPHERD ME, LORD
Daily Reflections for Your Lenten Journey

Printed in the United States of America by My Catholic Faith Press, P.O. Box 24886, Federal Way, WA 98093.

Cover Design by Jonny Georgeson.

Book Layout by Sharon Fox

ISBN: 978-0-9884791-1-1

INTRODUCTION

"Shepherd Me, Lord, into this Lenten Desert"

Lent is a liturgical season. We mark time on our liturgical calendar differently than we do in the typical calendar that we follow daily. And part of the insight that we can take from this difference, from the standpoint of faith, is to recognize that the Lord intervenes in history—He breaks in. There's a sense of immediacy we each experience this Lenten season.

I'd like you to consider the following: you have only one chance to live this Lent. Also, consider further that the Lord has been waiting for this Lent for all eternity; He has been waiting for this Lent to occur within your life. He intends to shepherd you through a desert that has your name on it in order to bring you through to a Promised Land of good things—the blessings He has set aside for you this year.

As you enter into this Lenten season, say to the Lord, "What is this Lent to be about in my life; what do you want to do in my life during this Lenten season? I desire to say 'yes' to all that you have in store for my Lent this year. Shepherd me, Lord, into the desert—this Lenten desert—that has my name on it, for I do not want to miss the graced moment of this liturgical season."

ASH WEDNESDAY

Understanding, Connection, and Participation

Drudgery—not a very nice sounding word, is it? But that's what you should expect in your experience of this Lenten season unless three things apply: *understanding, connection,* and *participation.* I could spend a lot of time with my kids reinforcing the idea that boredom is expected whenever they pray the rosary or go to Mass—that is, until they 1) *understand* what the Mass or the rosary is all about (or a certain part of the Mass or mystery of the rosary they're currently engaged in); 2) *connect* to the Mass or the rosary so they can feel a sense of meaningfulness between these traditions and that which is happening in their own lives; and 3) most of all, realize that they are *participating* in prayer and celebration with the Lord.

Think of a person who has never attended a soccer game before. They go to a game; if they don't understand the rules, they'll probably get bored. But let's say they understand soccer; if they don't have any connection to any of the players or the teams, they may not be as likely to be engaged. However, the most engaged person in a soccer game is always the player on the field, the one *participating* in the game itself. Lent is a lot like soccer—if we understand it, if we feel a sense of connection to it, and if we realize the ways the Lord draws us into a deeper level of participation with Him, then that's when Lent moves out of drudgery and into deep transformation. This is what the Lord intends for us this Lent.

I hope that you will walk with me through this Lenten journey, and in doing so, experience new levels of understanding, connection, and participation in the great work the Lord intends to do in your life. Let's follow Him and see what happens.

THURSDAY AFTER ASH WEDNESDAY

We are Dust and Into Dust We Shall Return

"Remember, man, that thou art dust and into dust thou shalt return." (Gen. 3:19) Today is Thursday. If you went to Mass yesterday on Ash Wednesday then you heard those words spoken at the moment when ashes were applied to your forehead. What's the meaning behind this symbolic gesture? Why do we do this at the start of our Lenten season? We must first understand the ashes. Where do these ashes come from? The ashes are from the palm leaflets that were used during the previous Lent celebration of Palm Sunday. Palm Sunday is that event when Jesus enters victoriously into Jerusalem, hailed as King. Then five days later, he is lifted up on the cross and, in the Gospel of John, is identified there as "King of the Jews." The ash connects us back to Palm Sunday; it connects the path of Jesus' passion, death, and resurrection to our own Lenten journey. These palms were crushed and burned; their ashes were applied to our foreheads. They weren't simply smeared either, they were applied in the sign of the cross.

Ash Wednesday is the beginning of our Lenten journey through which we are asked to walk with the Lord—a path that will lead to the cross. Not just to the cross but *through* the cross to His glorious resurrection on Easter Sunday. And so today let's reflect upon yesterday's event, when ashes were applied to your forehead in the sign of the cross: "Remember that you are dust and to dust you shall return." You, who have humble beginnings, have been invited by the Lord to accompany Him on a path through passion and death and into resurrection to a new life. You've been invited to a destiny that is literally beyond this world, and to sharing in God's own life forever in heaven. That's the journey you are on this Easter.

FRIDAY AFTER ASH WEDNESDAY

Bringing Life Out of the Lifeless

Growing up in Boston, prior to the spring equinox one could walk outside and look upon things that appeared dead and lifeless; the trees were a mesh of sticks and twigs; there were no buds, no blooming. The time before spring was a time when things seemed barren.

The word "Lent" comes from an Old English word meaning "springtime." What does springtime exactly mean? Springtime is a time when that which appears to be dead springs back to life. If we define springtime as such, then the meaning we hold close to us will help us understand what it is the Lord intends to do in our lives this Lent.

You may see at first the totality of your spiritual life, or perhaps some parts of your spiritual life, as appearing dead. The Lord sees deeper than this; He knows that within you is a capacity. What is this capacity? It is His own power to bring that which appears lifeless (or truly is lifeless) back to life. The Lord intends for you, in this Lenten journey, to bring out life from that which appears lifeless. Open your heart today, to the Lord and all that He wants to bring to life in you as you walk with Him through this Lent.

SATURDAY AFTER ASH WEDNESDAY

Prune in Order to Bloom

My wife Kari loves to grow flowers. She loves to plant certain parts of our yard with annuals and perennials; perennials are flowers that return year after year. And among all these kinds of flowers, roses are her favorite. One of the things that I've noticed, watching her tend her garden, is her annual springtime ritual of pruning these rosebushes, cutting them back. I'm not very familiar with the process of tending a garden. So the first time I saw her go out to prune the rosebushes, I thought she was destroying them. She cut them back so extensively that there was barely anything left. I asked her what she was doing. She said, "Tom, prune in order to bloom. I want these roses to bloom in a way that will allow them to truly flourish. These plants can then grow to their full potential over time; so I have to be somewhat ruthless in my pruning." *Be ruthless in the pruning for the sake of the blooming.*

Welcome to Lent, my friends. The Lord loves us and intends for us to bloom spiritually as His beloved sons and daughters to send us forth—to radiate forth—His glory in this world. In Lent He invites us to undergo His process of pruning so that we might bloom to our full spiritual potential. Lent is a journey; it's springtime. The Lord intends to bring life out of that which appears lifeless. And one of the most important activities that lead us to bloom is pruning.

Beginning next week, in our reflections we'll take a look at three fundamental ways the Lord invites you to undergo this pruning: prayer, fasting, and almsgiving. For the moment, pray for the willingness to undergo the pruning that the Lord has set aside for you this Lent.

FIRST SUNDAY OF LENT

Lenten Sundays as Mini-Easters

What are you giving up for Lent? That's a question that I was asked quite often growing up in a Catholic home and having many Catholic friends. Chocolate, popcorn, TV—you know how the list goes. What are *you* giving up for Lent? That's not a bad thing to consider.

One of the things that we looked forward to as kids during Lent was Sunday. On Sundays we got to enjoy those things we had given up for Lent. On Sundays we didn't experience Lent in the same way that we experienced it on the other days of the week. What do I mean by this? We think of Lent as being forty days long, but if we count it out on a calendar from Ash Wednesday to Easter Sunday, we get a higher number. Why?—because Sundays aren't counted. Sundays aren't experienced in Lent in the same way as Monday through Saturday. Sunday is a mini-Easter. Even in the midst of this journey with the Lord through the desert, the Lord gives us a temporary refreshing oasis.

I encourage you to discern whether the Lenten practices that you feel called to embrace are practices that you might give up on Sunday as well—as a means of acknowledging and celebrating Easter for which we give up many things. We celebrate Easter a bit on every Sunday in Lent as a means of anticipating the great celebration on Easter Sunday.

MONDAY OF THE FIRST WEEK OF LENT

Being Led into the Desert this Lenten Season

What does it mean to participate in Lent? I want to reflect on that a little bit. In our liturgical season we are invited to accompany Jesus on his forty-day journey into the desert. That's one of the scriptural references which have a meaningful application to Lent. And it's the primary reference. If we reflect on some of the details of the story of Jesus being in the desert for forty days, we'll then understand more fully what it is the Lord wants to do in our lives.

I want to draw attention to the first element that shows up in the story of Jesus going into the desert: Jesus doesn't decide first of all to go into the desert; rather, he is *led* into the desert. The Holy Spirit has come upon him in a special way at his baptism. The Father speaks, "This is my beloved Son, in whom I am well pleased." (Matt. 3:17) It's after that moment of Jesus' baptism that he is suddenly pushed—as some gospels put it—driven, or led into the desert.

Consider that this Lenten season is less about you deciding what you intend to give up; it's less about you making a choice about what sort of path you'll take. And it's more about you being open, receptive, docile, and ready to be led into that desert the Lord has set aside for you. Pray that you would be open to being led by the Holy Spirit into that desert that has your *name* on it. And remember that you too share in, and in some way experience, Jesus' journey of being led into the desert by the Holy Spirit in His life. That's what our Lenten journey is all about.

TUESDAY OF THE FIRST WEEK OF LENT

The Goal of Our Journey into the Desert

Jesus is baptized, he goes into the desert for forty days, and then he returns and is seen entering public ministry. He goes forth to proclaim in a public way the coming of God's kingdom. Let's connect that reality in Jesus' life to our own lives. Just as we are invited to be led by the Holy Spirit into the desert that has our name on it, we must also *not* lose sight of the goal at hand. The Lord intends for us a transformation so that we will be better equipped, empowered, and readied to proclaim, to be public witnesses, and to be ones sent forth by Christ into the world in this moment. Jesus, the one who lives within us and who accompanies us into the desert, wants to live through us in this world. We are to be his hands and his feet, says St. Teresa of Avila. We are to be salt and light, says the Lord. He intends to have us shine in this world. It's helpful to remember this ultimate goal as we undergo our own journeys through the desert.

It's not easy being in the desert. What helps is realizing this goal and keeping it in sight. Why are you going into the desert? It's for the sake of being equipped and readied to bear fruit in ministry once your Easter season arrives.

Poverty, Purity, and Humility

The People of Israel's forty-year journey through the desert is another scriptural association we can make. Moses shepherds God's people out of bondage in Egypt through the desert and into the Promised Land. This is another way for us to reflect and think about this season of Lent. The Lord himself intends to set us free from the bondage of sin and other forms of spiritual and moral slavery that we experience in our everyday lives. He intends to speak the truth that we will be freed from this bondage, and our entry into the Promised Land will be prepared. But what happens to God's people in the desert? They learn to rely on Him there, to be led by Him, and to be humbly at His service.

When encountering the reality of the desert on your Lenten journey, you are stripped of what you are attached to, and thus you acknowledge your fundamental poverty before God. You are stripped of your own willfulness, and you strive for a purity of intention. And finally, you are led by God's Holy Spirit when you humbly acknowledge God as the God of your life, allowing Him to overthrow any idols you may put before Him. The three fundamental virtues for the Christian life—poverty, purity, and humility—are the fruits of your being led through the desert in Lent.

Pray for these virtues: pray for poverty of spirit, purity of intention in every dimension, and a humility that is a praiseworthy self-abasement before God. May He raise you up as you enter into the Promised Land, the goal of your God-established journey.

THURSDAY OF THE FIRST WEEK OF LENT

God as It Were, Appealing through You

"We are ambassadors for Christ. God as it were, appealing through us." (2 Cor. 5:20) This comes from the second reading of the liturgy of the word at Mass on Ash Wednesday. God wants to appeal through you; that's what Lent is all about. And if you take a look at the two scriptural parallels we have focused on—Jesus' journey through the desert and God's people led by Moses in their journey through the desert—notice the role of the Holy Spirit. The Holy Spirit, who comes upon Jesus at his baptism and who pushes Him into the desert, is the supernatural intervention of God, who also sets free God's people from Egypt. The Holy Spirit accompanies God's people, appearing in a cloud by day and a pillar of fire by night. Being led by the Holy Spirit is cleansing, and this prepares them for entry into the Promised Land.

Jesus, after enduring the temptations that occur in the desert, comes into the synagogue to begin His public ministry; He reads from Isaiah 61: "The Spirit of the Lord is upon me; he has anointed me." The one who does great work in all of us is the Holy Spirit.

What the Holy Spirit does within God's people in the time of Moses and what the Holy Spirit does in the life of Jesus is the same as what the Holy Spirit does in your own life—given to you at baptism, poured out in an increased and fresh new way in confirmation. The Holy Spirit wants to lead you through this Lent so that you will be an ambassador for Christ: *God as it were, appealing through you.*

FRIDAY OF THE FIRST WEEK OF LENT

More Than an End, Also a Means

Lent is considered a season of penance and penitence. But among all the days that we experience in Lent, Fridays have a particular focus on acts of penitence such as fasting and other forms of self-denial. One of the important things to remember about Lent is that walking with Jesus through the desert, which we do spiritually during Lent, isn't simply an end in itself, but also a means.

Remember the pattern: first, the Holy Spirit falls upon Jesus and His baptism and moves Jesus into the desert; then, Jesus is led by the Spirit for forty days for the sake of his entry into public ministry; and finally, Jesus comes out of the desert and shows up at the synagogue to announce that the Spirit of the Lord is upon Him. The same pattern is at work in the story of Moses, who by God's intervention leads God's people out of slavery in Egypt. They're guided by the Spirit through the desert for forty years in order to enter into the Promised Land; and when they finally reach the Promised Land, they become God's faithful people.

Today as you go about your day in fasting and abstinence and self-denial, remember that these are acts that you do not perform simply as goals in and of themselves, but also as means of stripping, cleansing, and preparing you to enter more fully into the world as one of God's people and as one of His holy witnesses.

SATURDAY OF THE FIRST WEEK OF LENT

Becoming Ready and Useful for the Lord

"We are ambassadors for Christ; God as it were, appealing through us." (2 Cor. 5:20) This striking sentence, which you may remember, comes from Paul's second letter to the Corinthians. I reference it here, as we continue through the Lenten season, as a reminder that from the very beginning the Church wants to give us some sense of the goal, some idea of where we're headed. The call that God has for you at the end of this Lenten journey is that you will be more fitting, more profoundly usable by God as His messenger through whom God aims to appeal.

How will Lent help you become this ambassador through whom God can appeal more fully? Let me paraphrase a bit the following text written by Hans Urs von Balthasar; when you think of what Lent is, think of this text: *Our call is to strive constantly to dredge out the soul, to make it more and more ready for God—a burning readiness to be used and consumed for the salvation and redemption of the world.* That's the desire that should be driving you through Lent—a desire to have your soul dredged out of all that muddies the life-giving water of the Spirit who is at work in you, and all that holds back the appeal that God would make through you.

Beg the Lord today for a deeper yearning, for a deeper desire, for a burning desire, to be ready and useful for God's purposes, for God's appeal through you in this world.

SECOND SUNDAY OF LENT

Rest in His Arms of Love

When you look at the Church's liturgical calendar you see seasons like Advent and Christmas. You also see certain days that call for fasting or feasting. Today is the second Sunday in our Lenten journey. As in the previous Sunday, this too is a mini-Easter, and as such it's a day when you can fittingly set aside those acts of self-denial, penance, and penitence. Consider today an oasis.

But maybe it's not simply about giving up these things, but giving yourself over to the one for whom you give up these things. In other words, consider this a day of refreshment during which you enjoy your relationship with the Father and His love for you in a new way. It's not simply about not doing things, it's about turning to the one whom you love, turning to the one who loves you, and giving Him a chance to pour His love into you, to come close to you in a new way, in a new depth, at a new level.

So today, during this Sunday rest, rest in His arms. Don't just rest from the fasting and acts of self-denial, rest in His arms of love, rest and remain in that love. Let today be that day of rest. And if you do that, you will discover refreshment—a fresh energy and a fresh willingness to enter back into those very acts of self-denial, of penitence, abstinence, and fasting that you have willingly embraced during this liturgical season.

What the Lord Intends to Form Within Us

When we reflect on the scriptural accounts of Jesus in the desert, the story that stands out to us most prominently is the account of Jesus being tempted by the devil. The three temptations are to turn stones into bread, leap off the roof of the temple, and fall down in worship of Satan. These three temptations provide a mirror, an opportunity for you to reflect upon three fundamental attitudes the Lord desires to form within you as a disciple of his Son. Those three fundamental attitudes of the spiritual life are poverty, purity—especially purity of intention—and humility.

Poverty, purity, and humility—these three fundamental attitudes aren't necessarily the first things we pursue wholeheartedly. In the days to come, reflect more fully upon those three fundamental attitudes and how the Lord may form them within you this Lenten season. Pray for the openness to be led by the Lord this Lent into situations He may use as a means of forming within you a deeper poverty, purity, and humility.

TUESDAY OF THE SECOND WEEK OF LENT

The Three Temptations of Christ

First, Jesus is tempted to turn stones into bread. The Scriptures recount that after forty days and forty nights of fasting in the desert, Jesus has grown very hungry. Thus, the devil first tempts Jesus in His moment of extreme hunger, calling upon Jesus to use his own power to turn stones into bread in order to fulfill His hunger. But Jesus chooses spiritual poverty; He chooses to remain in a place of powerlessness; He chooses to remain in a place of incapacity rather than exercising His power. Spiritual poverty—that's the first attitude Jesus displays in overcoming this temptation. He refuses to give in to His own hunger, refusing to sustain Himself through His own power, and instead remains powerless before the Father's own power. He awaits the power of God—His providential care.

Second, Jesus is tempted to forgo purity of intention. The devil brings Jesus to the roof of the temple and tests Him: "Throw yourself off the temple; angels will clearly save you from falling and hurting yourself." (Matt. 4:6) But Jesus, with the purity of intention, refuses to put God to the test. He refuses to make a spectacle in Himself in the course of accomplishing God's mission in the desert. Instead, Jesus chooses to endure the test, rather than putting God to the test.

And third, Jesus is tempted into controlling the outcome of His mission by taking power into his hands through an act of betrayal: turning away from the Father to worship the devil. But he chooses instead to remain humble, lowering himself before his Father so that the Father would lift him up in the way He intends in order to accomplish the work with which Jesus is tasked.

Jesus knows and lives poverty of spirit, purity of intention, and absolute humility before his Father as the means by which He overcomes the temptations of Satan. He also maintains his identity, fulfilling His mission as the Son of God, Savior of the world. You, as a follower of the Lord in this Lenten journey, are asked to embrace Jesus in these three attitudes of poverty, purity, and humility.

Now pray that as you face your own tests, trials, and temptations which come your way, you too will embrace these gifts of God, these three attitudes.

WEDNESDAY OF THE SECOND WEEK OF LENT

The Spectacular Benefits of Fasting

Jesus is tempted to turn stones into bread due to extreme hunger after fasting for forty days and forty nights. During our Lenten journey, the Church only requires us to fast on Ash Wednesday and Good Friday while the other Fridays of Lent are days of abstinence. But the recommendation is that we discern, in our own life circumstances, how the Lord asks us to fast.

One of the ways that we might find an inspiration to embrace further fasting in Lent is to look at the power that comes from fasting, as recounted in Scripture. Moses fasts before he has his encounter with God on Mount Sinai, which leads to the entrustment of the Ten Commandments, which Moses delivers to God's people. Elijah fasts while on the mountain in the cave prior to encountering the Lord in a gentle breeze. Daniel fasts when he's thrown into the lions' den and is thus preserved from the harm. Jonah preaches repentance to the people of

Nineveh, who then repent and fast in sackcloth and ashes; they ward off punishment for their sinful ways. John the Baptist lives a life of fasting, eating locusts and wild honey, and comes out of the desert capable of recognizing the Messiah and preparing the way for the Lord.

We shouldn't consider these scriptural examples as things simply relegated to the past. Pope Paul VI uses these passages from Scripture to point out that fasting has been shown in our tradition to be a means of preparing us for encountering God, like Moses. Fasting disposes us for deeper prayer, like Elijah. It protects us in times of danger, like Daniel. It also enables us to express deep penitence for our own sins, like Jonah. And, lastly, fasting provides us with a keen eye to recognize the Lord in our midst so that we may prepare the way for the Lord, like John the Baptist.

These are just some of the spectacular benefits that come from fasting. Take some time to consider these benefits. You may find that you are motivated to embrace a degree of fasting further than what's required during your Lenten season. Fasting can truly equip you to be a powerful disciple of the Lord.

THURSDAY OF THE SECOND WEEK OF LENT

Fasting: a Relationship to Ourselves

As a spiritual discipline, fasting goes along with prayer and almsgiving. And as spiritual disciplines, they are connected to relationships. For instance, it's obvious that prayer as a discipline in Lent concerns our relationship with God and that almsgiving concerns our relationships with others. The word "alms" is expressive of a way of extending ourselves in love towards others. But then there's fasting. Fasting isn't about extending ourselves toward anything external; it's about diminishing ourselves. Through fasting, we learn to restrain ourselves for the sake of our relationship with God.

So as you continue to reflect on fasting, remember that fasting as a discipline is about a relationship. Prayer extends your relationship towards God, almsgiving extends your relationship towards others, and fasting in a certain way helps you to foster a more life-giving relationship towards your own body, towards yourself.

Joining with Christ in Redemption through Fasting

Although today, Friday, in Lent is not a day of formal fasting, it is a day of abstinence—from meat. However, Fridays are still a very fitting day for fasting. Why?—because Fridays link us to Jesus Christ and his passion and death on the cross. So many of our acts of penitence and repentance are expressive of our recognition that we have failed the Lord. Fasting can be a discipline that links us to the saving act of the Lord. Fasting as an act of self-denial is a way of joining spiritually in the supreme act of self-denial—Jesus' death on the cross. And so, a deep spiritual meaning of fasting can be: "I say 'no' to myself in order to say 'yes' to my union with Jesus." He denied himself for the sake of us; He died so that we might live.

You fast today as an act of self-denial so that Jesus might live in you more fully. Through his act of redemption for the whole world, you may now join

Him in your own act of redemption through fasting. That's the ultimate meaning of fasting for your spiritual life. It becomes a concrete way for you to express the union that you long to have with your crucified Lord. I invite you to fast as a way of expressing your loving desire to express the union that is yours with your Lord.

SATURDAY OF THE SECOND WEEK OF LENT

Fasting Will Reveal the Hunger of My Heart, My Spirit

Fasting is about extending yourself in this spiritual discipline in the way that you relate to your body. Not only is fasting an act of penitence, an act of self-denial, but it's an act that will reveal to you your own relationship to your body and the urges that live within it. When you fast, you are choosing to be intentional about when you eat and what you eat. Your body doesn't have a lot to say about that.

During the course of your day, if you've chosen to eat a small amount of food for breakfast and lunch, your body will say, "Hey! What's going on here?" Your body will speak to you about the desires that live within it for satisfaction. And if you stay true to the discipline of fasting, you're going to learn quite a bit about how strongly attached you are to satisfying the urges of your body. But at a deeper level, fasting will reveal to you the hunger that exists within your soul, the hunger of your spirit for God and for His word. It's a hunger for that Word that comes from God; it's Jesus himself that truly satisfies the deepest longings of your heart, the deepest longings of your being. But when you fully satisfy the urges of your body, oftentimes the deeper hungers of your soul remain hidden from you. Fasting is a wonderful cure for that.

As you fast, not only will you begin to diminish the attachment that your body has to food, it will also strengthen the will that you have to say "no" to the unconscious cravings of your body. Fasting will then begin to reveal to you in a new way, at a new depth, the true hunger that exists in your heart. What a powerful gift you have been given in the act of fasting.

THIRD SUNDAY OF LENT

Uncovering in Order to Heal

On this third Sunday of Lent, the gospel story of the Samaritan woman, who meets Jesus at the well, is read at Mass. It's also on this Sunday that the elect, those who are entering the Church, experience the first of three scrutinies. A scrutiny is a very interesting ritual in which the elect uncover through questioning those parts of themselves that are broken or trapped in sin and in need of healing. Scrutiny is something that we tend to want to avoid in our lives—"Don't let too bright a light shine upon my life." But the gospel of the Samaritan woman should give us hope. Jesus uncovers her in order to heal her; he uncovers her eyes through dialogue. And through their exchange, he is able to cast meaningful scrutiny on her life. She comes to experience salvation through the recognition that Jesus wants to bring her life-giving water. He knows her down to the core of her being—"He told me everything that I had ever done." (John 4:29) She goes and proclaims; she experiences the uncovering, the scrutinizing that unveils those weakest parts in order to heal.

I invite you to ask the Lord to scrutinize your life to uncover before your own eyes those areas of your life that are broken, damaged, in need of healing, and trapped in sin. Jesus wants to uncover these things to you precisely because he wants to heal you, strengthen you, and set you free.

MONDAY OF THE THIRD WEEK OF LENT

Thank God for Our Powerlessness

Before we finish with the concept of fasting as a spiritual discipline, I want to direct us back to the entry point for these reflections—Jesus' temptation in the desert to turn stones into bread. Here, we identify the spiritual attitude of poverty, or poverty of spirit. This is an attitude that marks our lives from the beginning. Thomas Aquinas says that we were created by God naturally—that is, with a nature possessing a goal, an endpoint, something beyond nature itself, something supernatural. That ultimate goal is our call to be children of God and to share in God's own divine nature.

Divinity is always infinitely beyond our mortal capacity. The only possible way for us to overcome this incapacity, this powerlessness, is through God's power of supernatural intervention in our own lives, which He graciously wills for us through his Son in the gift of his Spirit. While this is true with the foundation of our lives, it's also true as we attempt to live our lives as disciples of Jesus.

In this Lenten season, I encourage you to consider how it is you relate to the situations, times, and places in your own life in which you experience a sense of powerlessness, a sense of incapacity. In those moments, you perceive a chasm incapable of being crossed by your own will, your own strength. Instead of avoiding these chasms, thank God for them. They reveal to you the fundamental status that is yours; you are spiritually poor until God grants you the infusion of his power.

And so day-to-day, be careful about how you relate to situations of powerlessness; when you experience them, turn to the Lord and ask for His power. Spiritual poverty becomes the doorway through which God's power will be experienced by you. St. Paul said, "For when I am powerless, it is then that I'm strong." (2 Cor. 12:10)

TUESDAY OF THE THIRD WEEK OF LENT

PTPIA—Praise

One of the challenges I face as a father is teaching my children how to pray. I've discovered a simple five-letter acronym that helps my children grow in different ways in their lives of prayer: PTPIA—*Praise, Thanks, Petition, Intercession,* and *Asking* for intercession. I love to invite my kids to begin by praising God. The reason for that is when you praise God as our tradition teaches, especially our scriptural and catechistic traditions, we praise Him simply because God is God. We don't primarily praise Him for anything He has done for us in particular, but rather for who He is. Praising God sets us in the right direction. When we begin our prayer, with acts of praise, we begin extending ourselves towards God without any reference to ourselves.

During the Lenten season, I encourage you to incorporate more times of praise and worship into your prayer—times when you simply turn to the

Lord and praise Him; praise God for being God. If you find that to be a difficult or unfamiliar concept, then consider praising Him through song—either with songs of praise or reciting or singing the psalms. These can be powerful ways for you to direct the focus of your time of prayer away from yourself and fixate it on God. Remember, PTPIA begins with praise.

WEDNESDAY OF THE THIRD WEEK OF LENT

PTPIA—Thanks

When we think about thanks-giving, we might think of Mass, the perfect act of thanks-giving. Mass is the very way in which the Son of God performs His act of thanks to the Father. And through Him, with Him, and in Him we join in that perfect act of thanks. However, when we incorporate prayers of thanks-giving into our daily life, we will discover just how generous and merciful God is. God is a generous God, who has given us every good gift and fills us to overflowing. He blesses us when we ask Him, when we don't ask Him, and when we deserve the exact opposite. Our God is not only generous, He is also merciful. He is merciful in how He rescues us from those times and places in our lives when we have failed Him. He is merciful in that He preserves us from falling into sin and into other dangers. Our God is generous and merciful, and for that we should give Him thanks.

As you give thanks, you will come to know more fully who your God is, and you are much less likely to take things for granted. You may even get to that point where you discover that your God, who is greater than any circumstance that life can throw at you, can be thanked in every circumstance that life *does* throw at you. In the best of times and in the worst of times, give thanks to God. This is a very powerful and important way for you to extend yourself through the spiritual discipline of prayer during the Lenten season. Today, incorporate a time of giving thanks to God.

THURSDAY OF THE THIRD WEEK OF LENT

PTPIA—Petition

Many of the things that we're asked to do during Lent can be quite difficult. Petition is one particular form of prayer that I hope you'll embrace as part of your spiritual discipline of prayer. Remember the pattern of PTPIA: Praise, Thank, Petition, Intercession, and Asking for intercession.

Petition is when you ask God for a good thing for yourself, a blessing that you want for your own life. Your Heavenly Father is glorified when you ask Him for good things for your life. He wants to display to you just how much you are loved, and He wants to reveal to you just how good He is as your Heavenly Father. Material blessings, spiritual blessings, the blessings that you need for your life—bring these to Him with confidence. Ask boldly, for you are His beloved son or daughter because of the work of His son. He sent the gift of the Spirit to dwell within you so that you would come to discover that He is Abba—Father, Daddy.

You can come to know just how good God is to you when you take the risk of asking Him for the good things that you need in your life. If you're not sure what to ask for today or during the Lenten season, then ask God for two things: first, for the grace that you most need, and secondly, ask Him to bless you with the gift that would please Him the most. Those are two prayers, two petitions, He is certain to answer.

FRIDAY OF THE THIRD WEEK OF LENT

PTPIA—Intercession

Intercession is often where we first begin when we pray; intercession is asking for the sake of others, for the good of others. And intercession is an important way for us to pray; it's not primary, but it's important nonetheless. Intercession allows God to show that we, too, are involved in bringing about the blessings He intends for the world.

So often we relate to intercession as if we are bringing to God some situation that He might not be aware of; we ask Him to do something that maybe He hasn't considered, as if we're convincing Him to take action. But intercession is actually the opposite. Intercession is an act inspired by God in us; the Lord stirs you to pray for other people and situations wherever there is a need. He stirs you precisely because He wants to use your prayers as a conduit for, as a means of, in collaboration with, and as cooperation in, the very work He intends to do on earth. Your intercession allows the Lord to draw you in to a share in His heart to bring about good in this world. So intercede consistently, persistently, and courageously, because in doing so you're displaying back to God the very heart that He blesses the world with.

During this Lenten season, be generous in your intercession, because in doing so you will be used generously by God to bring about blessings on the earth.

PTPIA—Asking for Intercession

Prayer is that means by which we extend ourselves and our relationship to God. And I invite you again to embrace that helpful acronym, PTPIA: praising God, thanking God, petitioning God, interceding on behalf of others before God, and lastly asking for intercession. I love to incorporate asking into how I teach my kids to pray. Why?—because when my kids ask for intercession, it makes clear the reality of the relationship between heaven and earth. More precisely, the saints in heaven are connected to us on earth. And so when I ask my kids to ask for intercession as part of their prayer, they are given the opportunity to sense a connection. They sense that their prayers are joined with the prayers of a saint or saints in heaven. By asking for intercession, my kids will grow in their awareness of this relationship, and so will you.

Heaven sees earth even when we on earth can't see heaven—you too will discover this. You'll gain an increased awareness of the relationship existing between you and your patron saint, guardian angel, the saint whose feast day coincides with your birthday, or some other particular saint who maybe shares a common theme or bond with your life.

One of the powerful fruits of asking for intercession is developing a relationship with a saint or saints in heaven. I ask my kids not only to praise and thank, not only to petition and to intercede, but to courageously ask other saints in heaven for their intercession.

Consider in your prayer this Lent what saint or saints you feel a connection with, whom you would like to ask for intercession.

FOURTH SUNDAY OF LENT

"Lord, I am Blind; Help Me See"

"How can that person do that? Do they realize how they come across?" How many times do you confide that statement to a good friend or your spouse at a party or at home or on the way home? "Do they have any idea how they came across?" And the answer is likely: No. That person whom you're referring to simply doesn't see. They are blind, unable to see the severity of their attitude or the inappropriateness of their action or words. Sin has that same effect—it blinds us to it.

Today on this fourth Sunday in Lent, you will see a number of people at Mass, among the elect who are awaiting full entry into the Church. They will be scrutinized once again. This scrutiny is connected to the Gospel of John, in which the blind man is approached by Jesus and is led on a path to sight. Jesus, by being the light of the world, brings a light into our own lives so that we might move from blindness into sight.

Today, you can become aware, become conscious, and come to see that there are parts of your life to which you, too, are blind. There are moments in which you aren't aware of how you come across to others and don't recognize just how inappropriate or disturbing your attitudes, actions, or words are.

Pray that the Lord's light will unveil to you those areas where there is darkness, and that His light will indeed heal you so that you may become a more faithful transmitter—a conduit of Christ's light into this world. *Lord, I acknowledge that I am blind; help me see.*

MONDAY OF THE FOURTH WEEK OF LENT

Extending Ourselves toward Others

When we hear the word "almsgiving," what do we think about? Money, usually. Yes, almsgiving has to do with our own willingness to give money to others or to some charitable cause. But almsgiving actually has as its root meaning a word that means love. Almsgiving has to do with extending ourselves out of love in a way that is beyond what we normally might do the rest of the year. This liturgical season asks us to extend ourselves out of love.

These days, we often hear the Church, when remarking on offering (the notion of extending oneself towards others) as referring back to the concept of stewardship. When we are stewards, we're asked to give not only of our treasure (material wealth) but of our time and our talents. The same is true with regards to almsgiving. We can extend ourselves during the Lenten season in love toward those that are around us—family, friends, neighbors—by being willing to give of our time, our talents, and, yes, our treasure.

And so, as an entry point for this reflection, pray for openness to hear from the Lord a call to extend yourself out of love to your neighbor; for when you do that, you'll truly be encountering Christ, the one who is the goal of all of our journeys.

TUESDAY OF THE FOURTH WEEK OF LENT

Giving Time to Others

When we think about prayer, developing a relationship with God, the concept of spending time alone with God immediately jumps to the surface. Unless I spend time with God, how else can I nurture greater communication with God, develop a more intimate relationship with God, and express the love in my heart for God? Being more generous with time in prayer is a very natural way to express a sense of extending oneself towards God. The same is true with regards to our neighbors, as in loving others well. Be willing to give more generously of your time to others. It's a true act of almsgiving whether that means spending more time with your spouse, your kids, or your relatives or close friends.

But consider also spending more time with people who seem socially needy. I'm referring to people who have difficulty connecting with others or seem to have few friends. Perhaps they're new to the area or are in a state of bereavement. Perhaps they're naturally introverted and thus find communicating and developing relationships on the whole a bit more troublesome. Can you reach out to that person? Can you *not* walk away when that person approaches you? Can you be willing to give that person a bit more of your time to patiently, kindly, generously open yourself to receive that person in love as you would with others?

Ask the Lord, "Who can I extend myself to, extend myself towards in love, by spending more time with them?" God will help you discern who is in need of your time. If you ask God, if you consider the question, then I bet that person will appear in your mind, and you'll find yourself encountering that person very soon.

Pray that the Lord will give you a heart willing to spend more time out of love with someone—not with a begrudging attitude but with an openess which says, "Lord, when I relate to the least of these, my brothers and sisters, I am relating to you." Do that, and you'll be extending yourself to your neighbor not only out of your own love, but also out of love for God.

Who Would Benefit from Your Talents?

One of the customs that's becoming a bit more popular in the United States around Halloween is called "booing". In this custom you surprise a family member, neighbor, or friend with a gift amid the days leading up to Halloween. My wife Kari has come up with an alternative; she calls it "blessing". We put together a package of goodies such as a small box of candy, toys, puzzles, and other goodies. We give these "blessings" to other families, whom we anticipate being particularly blessed with such a gift around Halloween. Kari has a lot of fun getting our kids involved with these packages, having them accompany her when buying those goodies, putting the packages together, and figuring out which families we could extend ourselves toward to give these blessings.

You can also do this during Lent. You don't have to prepare a box of goodies, but consider what gifts the Lord has given you that you could extend to others.

What are you good at? What are your talents? Perhaps you're especially good at cooking or gift-wrapping. Maybe you're good at offering a particular service—tax season is here! What service can you provide to others—free of charge? Next, ask yourself: "Who would be particularly blessed by receiving my gift?" Do that.

What a great way to express a Lenten discipline—almsgiving. Don't only extend yourself by giving time and money, extend yourself also by giving of the talents God has graced you with. This is another way for you to be blessed, while also giving a blessing to others.

THURSDAY OF THE FOURTH WEEK OF LENT

Almsgiving—Being Generous with Our God-Granted Treasures

Being a good steward of our time and our talents are two ways we've reflected on almsgiving as a spiritual discipline during Lent—how we extend ourselves in love by giving of our time and our talents to others. It's important to look at the third call of almsgiving, being a steward of the treasure that God has put into our hands. Rather than offering practical tips about how we might extend ourselves by giving more of the treasure God has entrusted us with, consider instead how you *see* the treasure, the material wealth, which has been placed in your hands.

The Scriptures offer a wonderful cleansing perspective, converting the natural mindset we often discover in ourselves. The Scriptures say that we shall love the Lord our God with all our heart, souls, mind, and strength. The word, "strength," in Greek, is a way of referring to the wealth that we have in our possession. The reality of wealth is included in the ways we are called to love the Lord. All of the wealth that is in our hands comes from God. God is the source of all good things in our lives. The challenge is for us to recognize that we belong to God in every dimension of our being, including our material wealth and possessions.

Let's pray: "Lord, help me to love you by how it is I relate to this wealth. This wealth is yours just as I am yours; this treasure that is in my possession just happens to be in my possession—it belongs to you just as I belong to you. So grant me the grace this Lent to become ever more detached from a sense of ownership over the treasure that happens to be in my hands, and instead make me a faithful steward who has been entrusted with the charge over whatever wealth you have given to me. Give me the freedom to receive and the freedom to express generosity in how it is I share the wealth that is yours, which just happens to be in my hands."

Pray and reflect in this way, so that the Lord might grant you the grace you need to live out the stewardship of your finances when it comes to almsgiving this Lenten season.

FRIDAY OF THE FOURTH WEEK OF LENT

Growth in Holiness

Why aren't there more mystics today? A mystic is someone who receives very special graces from God, someone who advances along the paths of perfection in the spiritual life. Where are all the mystics? Well, our tradition might give us a bit of an answer, which is linked to some of the very practices we undertake during this special season of Lent. What do I mean? Since the Council of Trent in the 16th century, theology was taught for several hundred years through the use of manuals. One of the insights that this manual-approach to teaching theology brought about was the linkage between different themes in theology. For instance, teaching about God—there was a manual called *God is One,* which was taught alongside another one called *God is Three,* implying a very intimate connection between the two. This linkage also shows up when it comes to spiritual development. The course in mystical theology was taught alongside another manual—a course in *ascetical* theology. Asceticism comes from a Greek root word that has to do with training and disciplining. Undertaking spiritual disciplines particularly related to penance and penitence (putting to death the desires of the flesh so that the spirit might live) was intimately connected with spiritual development—growth in holiness or advancing in perfection along the stages of growth in holiness.

What does our tradition tell us? An age that disregards ascetical theology is cutting itself off from an essential part of the path of nurturing the mystical life. Do you want to be open, to be led to greater heights of holiness along the spiritual journey towards even greater mystical heights? Then prepare yourself to integrate as well.

Spiritual discipline is drawn from ascetical theology. What exactly does this look like? We will reflect on this connection in the days ahead. For now, hold on to that key insight drawn from our tradition. Growth in holiness involves both growth and graces that lead to spiritual development. The mystical path goes hand-in-hand with the path of ascetical or spiritual training, which is the putting to death in the flesh of all that leads away from God.

SATURDAY OF THE FOURTH WEEK OF LENT

Asceticism as Spiritual Practice for the Soul

"How do you get your kids to sit so still at Mass?" Kari and I will often encounter other parents asking us this question, because we have nine young kids, aged thirteen years to just a few months old. And although Kari and I will notice times when they aren't sitting as still as we think they should, other people will look upon our family and note how quiet and attentive our children are at Mass. The simple answer to the above question is that my kids practice being still at home. Ah! Asceticism! In other words, spiritual practice—undertaking spiritual disciplines that will help us advance in the spiritual life.

There's a relationship between what's happening in our bodies and what's happening in our souls, or spirits. I want you to think about how we recognize how the states of our bodies impact our souls. For example, the best time to pray probably isn't after a meal since our bodies are full and sleepy, and we lose concentration. This relationship also appears in our ability to be still and attentive at Mass. Undertaking a bit of spiritual training, some ascetical practices, such as having your kids learn how to be still during times of silence at home, can be an aid in helping them prepare for being still at Mass. Asceticism links that which occurs in our own bodies to what the Lord is doing in a deeper dimension at the level of our spirits—and this relationship is recognized when we prepare your bodies through ascetical practices to the Lord's work within our souls.

And so during this Lenten season, reflect upon how you relate what happens in your body, how you train your body, and also what happens in your soul. By reflecting more fully on the meaning of asceticism, spiritual training, you will gain deeper insight into how to live your spiritual life. It will mean much more than not praying after a meal or being still during quiet time outside of Mass. It will mean much more than that.

FIFTH SUNDAY OF LENT

"Unbind Him and Let Him Go Free"

During this fifth Sunday of Lent, the Church traditionally reflects on the gospel depicting Jesus raising Lazarus from the dead, in John chapter 11. Pay attention to the very end of this gospel at which point Jesus has called Lazarus by name; Lazarus then comes forth from the tomb. But that's not where the story ends. Jesus speaks to the others and says, "Unbind him and let him go free." (Jn. 11:44) Even though he's resuscitated, brought back to life, Lazarus is still bound up in the burial cloth, which would have covered him from his toes over his head and down along the length of his back. That single piece of burial cloth would have been tied together by individual bands of cloth around his body at various places. And so, Lazarus must have sort of wiggled and waddled his way out of the tomb, bound tightly by the burial cloth.

When Jesus says, "Unbind him and let him go free," the people around them would have had to come in, one at a time, and begin unbinding him from these restrictive pieces of cloth. This scene is like our Lenten journey; this story is very much like ascetical practices. By undertaking spiritual training, disciplining ourselves, we will unbind and set free those different aspects of our lives in which we are restricted, refraining from the sort of movement the Lord would desire for us to have. The Lord asks us to be willing to undergo ascetical practices as a means of accompanying with and cooperating in His good work and in our own growth in holiness.

Unbind him and let him go free. You may say “yes” to that in many ways. One of the ways you can say “yes” today is through ascetical practices.

Two Directions of Asceticism in the Spiritual Life

When we consider how the Church reflects on asceticism in the spiritual life, we find emphasis in two directions. First, there's positive emphasis on active self-restraint. Part of spiritual training is our active efforts to restrain ourselves. This shows up in phrases like "fight the good fight" or "strip off the old man and put on the new man." These are ways of talking about growth in the spiritual life through active efforts to restrain ourselves or to fight against tendencies that show up in our lives. The second is through efforts of detachment—efforts by which we pronounce different aspects of our lives, those parts that tend away from God, which are known as "the flesh". These are efforts to deny ourselves; these are efforts to mortify those passions that live in us, even to crucify those passions associated with the flesh. The Church uses language that goes in these two directions.

What we will do over the next two days is reflect on both efforts—the specific efforts that you can make to be active in fighting the good fight and in stripping yourself of those elements in your life that are reflective of the old man. You will also understand more fully what it means to renounce, deny, crucify, and mortify. How do these things show up in your life? This is where our reflections will go, to help you to understand more fully what the Church is asking of you or what the Church recommends to you, as you engage in ascetical practices.

TUESDAY OF THE FIFTH WEEK OF LENT

How Do We Engage in Active Self-Restraint?

How do we engage in a positive element of active self-restraint, of fighting the good fight and stripping off the old man so that the new man might shine forth? This is something that the Scriptures in our tradition draw attention to with great urgency. Saint Peter says, "As obedient sons, do not yield to the desires that once shaped you and your ignorance, but be holy yourselves in every aspect of your conduct after the likeness of the Holy One who called you." (1 Pet. 1:14) That's very striking. Thomas á Kempis in *The Imitation of Christ* says that one of the reasons we're held back in spiritual growth is a refusal to fight. St. Thomas Aquinas says that the virtue of magnanimity is found in those who desire to extend themselves to do something great for God. *The Catechism of the Catholic Church* has an entire section called the "Battle of Prayer," which it begins by stating that prayer is a gift that also requires a determined effort on our part. Well, concretely, how do we respond to that?

We might hear calls that are very motivating such as, "I want to engage in fighting the good fight; I want to strip off those parts of my life that are settling for less. What do I do?" Also, "How do I respond?" The answer I have for you is *I have no idea;* but I do know that you need to discern it. You need to discern whether you are fasting enough or denying yourself sufficiently or giving up those creature comforts; or perhaps you're too quick to fall back into easy patterns of comfort.

"Am I a person who wants to always have my way, or am I willing to die unto myself?" These are questions that only you can answer. But you must ask them nonetheless. You need to search within your heart and say, "Am I someone who's fasting too much or too little? Am I someone quick to fight that good fight? Am I someone who's quicker at putting my energies into fighting other battles like growing in my career or cultivating a particular passion?" These are personal questions that require your discernment.

The last thing that I want to do is foster any sort of extreme response on the part of any of you. Yet at the same time, the opposite could be just as dangerous.

You could risk halting ascetical practices, those serious efforts to discern the ways in which you might be engaged in restraining and disciplining yourself so that the Spirit might come more alive in you. You want to avoid either side of falling off the path. What you need is discernment and wisdom to stay on the path to appropriately welcome active efforts to restrain yourself, active efforts to embrace asceticism as part of your growth and holiness.

WEDNESDAY OF THE FIFTH WEEK OF LENT

Detaching Ourselves as Owners; Embracing Our Stewardship

The other dimension of asceticism which may be identified as negative is the idea of removing. One way this shows up is through the concept of renunciation. We see it in the gospels. In Luke 14:33, Jesus says, "Every one of you that does not renounce all that he possesses, cannot be my disciple." Being a disciple of Jesus for every one of us involves renouncing everything we possess. Earlier in the gospel, Jesus called Peter, James, and John through this miraculous catch of fish; what happens when they reach the shore? "Abandoning their nets, they followed." This response is important for us today. The apostles renounce everything by leaving it behind. We today, when we make our active renunciation, renounce by leaving behind those elements in our lives that involve sin. But there is much in our life that we renounce ownership over while still retaining it as stewards.

Think of the fundamental relationships in your life. I, as a disciple of the Lord, when married to Kari, am called to renounce every relationship as secondary to my relationship with Christ. But when I put Christ first and renounce every other relationship from that first point, I retain Kari in my life. I relate to my children not as an owner but as a steward entrusted with the gift. Each child is a gift given from God.

This even shows up in practical things. What's something you possess that if asked to renounce, you would hesitate giving it away? How attached are you to that thing? "Am I the owner or the steward?" Your act of renunciation involves a renouncing forever of sin, while retaining as a steward the relationships and good things that God has given you. You are not attached to them as owner, but you are a grateful steward for the good things that God gives to you.

Renunciation: becoming detached and relating well to the good things that God has given to you. Find the balance; give back to God what He has given to you.

THURSDAY OF THE FIFTH WEEK OF LENT

Jesus Longs to Reign as King in Our Hearts

"If any man will come after me, let him deny himself and take up his cross and follow me"—Luke 9:23. This concept of self-denial is another way of expressing the Lenten challenge of asceticism as it involves detachment and self-denial. What is so striking about this concept is that we're not simply denying ourselves access to food via fasting or denying ourselves access to comfort and ease, which are things associated with our bodies. What we're actually asked to do is to deny our very selves: *I deny my own I.* Jesus asks us to give up first place in our own lives.

One way this challenge is reflected upon in popular spirituality is that there is one throne in your heart, and only room for one person to reign in your heart. And the question is: who gets to sit on the throne of your heart? Who gets to be king in your life? Self-denial is part of how scriptures describe the process of allowing Jesus to establish himself as King in our hearts. We deny ourselves not out of a sense of hatred for ourselves, not out of a lack of goodness, but rather because we have been named as "precious" and deemed as ones chosen by God to have his Son reign in us. You are so precious to God the Father that He considers you, we might say, territory worth conquering, over which Jesus longs to reign.

The most self-affirming and vivifying thing that you can do is to deny yourself that place in your heart and ask, welcome, and beg the Lord to come and reign as Lord in your heart. Self-denial in little things and big things is all about asking the Lord to come and reign as King upon that one throne that exists in the depths of your heart. Practice self-denial and let Him reign in your heart today.

FRIDAY OF THE FIFTH WEEK OF LENT

Putting to Death the Fallen Tendencies of Human Nature

In the Catholic tradition of ascetical theology, another concept stands alongside renunciation and self-denial; it's called mortification. Romans 8:13 states, "But if by the Spirit you mortify the deeds of the flesh, you shall live." It's important to note four different points presented in this text. The first is the concept of mortification itself. Mortification refers to the process of undergoing death. That doesn't sound very appealing. Who wants to undergo the process of death? But notice the other aspects of this text. The second is that it's the Spirit who leads this process of mortification. The Holy Spirit is involved in any work of authentic mortification. Third, mortification is connected to vivification, or coming alive—"you shall live." Thus, in the Christian journey, putting to death is part of how the Lord brings us to life. And fourth, what are put to death are the deeds of the *flesh*. The flesh, here, doesn't mean the body, it means those fallen tendencies of human nature that we all share—everything within us inclined toward sin.

So what is it that needs to be mortified, that needs to be put to death? It's not your body or yourself; it is the fallen tendencies of human nature. Those are the things that must be mortified in the course of your Lenten practices so that you might live.

Mortification is for the sake of coming alive, of vivification. The Holy Spirit leads you in this process and does so by putting to death those inclinations, those tendencies, those urges in your life that are associated with the fallen dimensions of human nature. These are issues we can all relate to. So take a moment to reflect and ask the Lord what deeds of the flesh He wants to put to death in your life today, so that He may bring you to life!

SATURDAY OF THE FIFTH WEEK OF LENT

Christ Crucified is the Center of Our Journey

"They that are Christ's have crucified their flesh with its vices and concupiscence" (Gal. 5:24). This Scripture passage points us to the ultimate foundation and the highest point of all of our ascetical practices. Any efforts that we make to detach ourselves, deny ourselves, or mortify ourselves in the end and at its highest point, must be connected to Jesus Christ and the path that he walked through his passion and death on the cross. Christ crucified is the center of our spiritual journey and becomes a focal point in our Lenten journey.

When you think of all those self-denying acts, giving up and putting to death those urges within you, remember that you don't do this apart from Christ. You don't do this in some kind of imitation *at a distance* from Christ. Rather, Jesus Christ, who longs for you to share in the resurrection of the new life and who has already begun that process of bringing that new life to birth through baptism, longs to bring this new life into full display. And that means, for you, a deeper union with Him on the cross.

The very acts that you do in Lent are connected with your active efforts and your willingness to be linked to Christ's crucifixion. This, for you, is the path to life. This, for you, is the path to Jesus Christ himself, risen from the dead, manifesting Himself in you. This is what He longs to do. He wills for you this crucifying journey through Lent so that the resurrected Christ might appear in your life. Look for ways that He is manifesting himself in your life and thank him for the privilege of sharing in His passion and death on the cross.

PALM SUNDAY

The Gap between Idea and Execution

Today is Palm Sunday; this is the day in which we remember Jesus Christ, coming as King into His holy city, to be among the chosen people. He was hailed with "Hosannas!" acknowledging him as king, and was greeted with waving palm fronds. But Jesus Christ himself comes to them in a humble way, riding a donkey.

There's a great difference in our lives between idea and execution. We have an idea in our minds, but when it comes to living it out, it's not always so easy. We can paint wonderful pictures in our minds of an ideal something that we would love to have happen. But then, when it comes to living it out, it's not always as simple as we imagine it, and we often fall short. The idea of these people, the chosen people, crying out that Jesus is King and welcoming him into their midst, is a beautiful one. That was their ideal. Sadly, five days later, because of the difficulty of welcoming him and the implications of hailing him as king in their midst, what began as a beautiful idea, ended with a brutal execution. On Good Friday, we witness their betrayal—those same people who cried out "Hosanna!" whose shouts turn into, "Crucify him! Crucify him!"

As we enter into Holy Week, let's pray for forgiveness from the Lord for all of those ways that that same gap—between our crying out, "Hosanna! I welcome you, Jesus, in the fullness of your kingship into my life!" and the actual execution - appears in our lives. When it comes to living out this idea, actually following him with fidelity day-to-day, then our idea, sadly, too often becomes an execution. Too often, we end up being counted among those who cry out, "Crucify him! Crucify him!"

This is the journey that you will walk this week during Holy Week. Be willing to welcome the full force of all that God has for you and all that God wants to reveal to you and in you of that gap that still exists between your beautiful idea and a brutal execution.

Pray, "Lord, may the true idea that you have for my life come to reality. May I put that into practice; may that be the journey of this Holy Week."

MONDAY OF HOLY WEEK

May We Be Cleansed Temples of the Holy Spirit

Several happenings in the life of Jesus are associated with Holy Monday. The two most prominent are the cursing of the fig tree and the cleansing of the temple. Both of these stories shine a bright light on your spiritual journey through Holy Week.

Jesus expects you to bear fruit. He comes upon a fig tree, and when He finds no fruit He curses the tree. Jesus has lavished you with every good gift—the gift of his Holy Spirit of baptism, faith, hope, and love, and so many other countless graces. He does so out of love for you; but He also does so because he has an expectation that you will bear fruit as His disciple who glorifies the Father.

He then cleanses the temple. He comes into *the* holy place and finds unworthy activity. And so He tips over the moneychangers' table because zeal for the House of the Lord consumes him. He is also zealous with His love, His desire that you also would be a cleansed temple of the Holy Spirit. As you continue your journey through Holy Week, don't fear but welcome the judgment of the Lord. He will gaze upon your life so that all that's within you that is not bearing fruit will wither and only that which *is* bearing fruit will remain. Welcome the Lord, who mercifully and out of His zealous love for you, enters into your temple—the temple of the Holy Spirit within you—and cleanses it of all unworthy thoughts, words, deeds, or omissions. This is your journey through Holy Week.

Holy Monday, traditionally called "Great Monday," is a day when the Lord draws near to you to judge amid your life all that is not bearing fruit, and cleanse in you all that is unworthy. Let Him complete His cleansing process in you today.

Light Shines through Our Good Deeds

Today is Tuesday of Holy Week. The Scripture traditionally associated with this day is the parable of the ten virgins, awaiting the arrival of the bridegroom. Jesus Christ is the bridegroom coming for his bride, the Church. And what He asks of us is that we be alert and awake, vigilant for His coming into our lives.

The parable of the ten virgins also points to the need we have to be living our faith through good works. Five of the virgins fall asleep; and when they do so, their lamps run out of oil. Oil, here, refers to good deeds. It is through good deeds that our light shines on this earth.

One of the ways that you will be vigilant in your life of faith is through seeking ways to let that faith shine through your actions, shine through your works, shine through your good deeds.

Vigilance is found not only in prayer but in the ways that prayer comes into your life; prayer must somehow come to birth in how you live your life of faith, for it is through this prayer-centered life that your light shines bright in this world. Being vigilant in prayer and being vigilant in living your faith are two ways that you can express the spirit of Holy Tuesday. Pray today for more vigilance in your life of faith and the power to live out your faith through good works.

WEDNESDAY OF HOLY WEEK

The Goal is in Sight

I've never run a marathon, but when I've asked people who have, "What's the most challenging mile to run?" they never say it's the final mile. They'll usually declare the toughest mile as being the 23rd, 24th, or 25th mile, because the end is not yet in sight, although they know it's near. This is very much like today, Wednesday of Holy Week. We're just about at the end of our Lenten journey, and yet, Easter Sunday still isn't quite in sight.

I encourage you not to stumble into the next three days; the Sacred Triduum is such an important part of our life of faith that I encourage you to take some time today to be practical in your reflection: *When will I go to Mass? How can I set my schedule aside so that I won't get so busy that I'll crowd out the impending holy moments?*

You're almost there, just about at the end of this Lenten journey. And for some of you, it might seem like it's been a marathon. But you are just about in sight of the goal. Do not stumble now; do not give up now. Take some time today to thank the Lord for how far you have come. Thank Him for laying before you the days to come, and pray to Him to identify those times and places and ways in which you can hold these next three days as truly coming from God. They are sacred. They are holy days.

HOLY THURSDAY

A Day, Overflowing

Holy Thursday is one of those beautiful feasts that shows how our life of faith is often marked by a *too-much quality*. There's so much beauty and bounty that it feels as if this day, like a vessel, will overflow. And so when you attend Mass today, you'll discover that the themes the Church invites you to reflect upon will fill you to overflowing. You are asked to reflect upon the establishment of the priesthood, the gift of the institution of the Holy Eucharist, and the visible reminder of the washing of feet. You will witness again Jesus' washing of his twelve apostles' feet. Jesus calls you to perform the same humble service in imitation of your Master.

There is so much here that a single day, Holy Thursday, struggles to contain it. I encourage you to enter into the *too-much quality* of your faith, and relish in, with great thanks-giving and praise, the gift of this day—the gifts of the priesthood, the institution of the Eucharist at the Last Supper, and the call to be a servant of all, in imitation of your Master.

GOOD FRIDAY

The Crucifixion: God's Glory Shining Forth

Today we celebrate a feast that has a name that might be difficult to understand; we call it Good Friday. And yet, on this day we commemorate the act which could appropriately be declared the worst ever committed by humanity: killing the innocent Son of God. The Church proclaims it Good Friday because it is the entry point into the greatest thing God has ever done. God turned death into life, turned creatures of earth into children of God, and freed those who would have been cut off from Him, delivering them into a destiny in which they can share life with God forever. This is what we celebrate on Good Friday.

Jesus, through His crucifixion, turns that which is the ugliest thing history has ever seen into a window through which God's glory shines at its greatest. This mystery is also something that should give you great hope, for you too share in times of suffering, in tragedies, and in deep, interminable moments of crisis and darkness. If God could turn the worst thing that humanity ever did into the moment in which His glory shines forth at its greatest, then He can do the same in your life. Take hope in that, especially when you are in a moment of suffering and darkness. Trust that He will turn your suffering into a moment in which His glory shines forth.

HOLY SATURDAY

Jesus Overcomes the Death of All

Today is Holy Saturday; it sits between Good Friday and Easter Sunday. It's an important moment of reflection for us in our spiritual lives. We often reflect during this day on how Jesus is with those who suffer. We also reflect on the reality of Easter Sunday—how Jesus overcomes death. But today it's also important to know that Jesus is in solidarity with those who are in the midst of death, who are experiencing the tragedy of loss.

In your life you will experience the reality of death. Today, reflect on the truth that Jesus knows more profoundly than any of us ever will, the reality of death. He has embraced on Good Friday not only suffering but also the deaths of all who will ever die. He has welcomed them into Himself so that the victory He displays on Easter Sunday is the overcoming of all death. Today, pause and thank the Lord for being with you even through the reality of death.

EASTER SUNDAY

Christ is Risen!

"Christ is risen!" This was the briefest way in the early Church of expressing the Good News. Why?—the fundamental situation of humanity is that we are alive, and we're facing the reality of death. As far as we can tell, all who are alive today will one day die, and those who are dead will stay dead.

The proclamation, "Christ is risen," is not only something good for Him (having overcome his own death) but good for all of us. Christ has overcome the death of all. All who are willing to join our lives to His will come to experience a new life won not for himself but for us through *His* death. "Christ is risen" inspires great hope that we too will go through death to share in a life as God's children. This is the God-willed destiny for our lives.

What you experience here on earth is just a foretaste of the true life that you were made for—the life God intends for you, to be with him forever in heaven. This is your joy and this is what you celebrate today. Your long journey through Lent is over. *Christ is risen!*

Pray that your destiny, which God intends to display in its fullest after your death, will display in your life here and now—more fully than ever before. Live the reality of Easter ever more fully as you live out your life here on earth!

Christ is risen! The Lord is risen indeed!

CONCLUSION:

"Thank you, Lord, for leading me to this graced moment"

We have crossed the desert, my friends, and found the Promised Land. We have walked with Jesus for forty days and forty nights, fasting, resisting the temptations of the devil, and returning back to the world to deliver the word of God and to let His light shine forth through us into the world. The ultimate goal of our Lenten journey, as I've stated before, is to be readied and equipped in order to be fruitful in ministry during this Easter season. Exactly how we're readied and by what ways we are equipped are both up to God, who has prepared each of us a desert with our name it.

We have considered on our journey new ways of deepening prayer -PTPIA: **praise, thanks, petitions, intercessions,** and **asking** for intercessions. We have considered the three Lenten virtues of **poverty, purity,** and **humility.** We have also reflected upon the ascetical disciplines of Lent, almsgiving, self-denial and self-restraint, as well as the scriptural parallels of journeying through the desert.

I hope that these reflections have aided you in opening up to God so that He may shine forth through you this Lenten season. Remember, in each journey of Lent, we walk not alone but with Christ, who wishes to speak through us, to heal us, to express through us God's greatest glories on earth. We are His children, shepherded through the desert to the Promised Land, to that Easter season in which we reflect upon Christ's death and resurrection.

Let Christ shine forth through your new, resurrected lives. Let the rigorous pruning you committed to this Lenten season, allow you to bloom to such a wonderful extent that would both please God and affirm His presence in your Life.

Let us pray: *Lord, you are the shepherd of my life. You have shepherded me through this Lenten season to the Promised Land of Easter. I recall now Jesus, your Son's death on the cross and resurrection. I have been led through many trials this Lenten season—honed, purified, and transformed through the rigors of fasting, self-restraint, and self-denial. Through this journey I have been equipped and readied in order to receive your Word, to receive Christ's eternal gift of salvation in my life, and to let shine forth during this Easter season and beyond, your saving light. Thank you, Lord, for using me as a vessel for this light, for setting me upon this desert I have crossed. Thank you, Lord, for leading me to this graced moment. Amen.*

The following is an excerpt from the opening pages of Dr. Tom Curran's best-selling book

THE MASS

Four Encounters with Jesus that will Change Your Life

INTRODUCTION

IS MASS BORING OR ARE WE?

Being Christian

is not the result of an ethical choice

or a lofty idea,

but the encounter with an event,

a person [Jesus Christ]

which gives life a

new horizon and decisive direction.

Pope Benedict XVI, *God is Love*

I love going to Mass. But I often hear, "Mass is boring. We say the same thing every Sunday; it doesn't make sense. Why should I go to Mass when I don't get anything out of it?" If you've ever found yourself saying these things or wondering what to say to someone who does, then please keep reading.

Do you go to Mass because you are supposed to but don't really understand what's going on? Do you have a hard time keeping your mind from wandering? Would you like the Mass to have a bigger impact on your life but you're not sure what to do about it? I wrote this book for you. Simply put, the Mass is not dull. We are dull. I know this first hand.

For years my mind was dulled by a lack of awareness. I didn't comprehend what was *really happening* at Mass, what was being *offered to me* and what was being *asked of me*. Too often I sat in the pew watching the priest like an uninterested spectator observing and occasionally reacting to what was happening on the field. Once I realized that the pew was part of the playing field, Mass became a lot less boring. At Mass, there are no seats for *spectators*. If you are there, even in a pew, you are in the game. Just as a football team is made up of players with different but uniquely important roles, at Mass you and I have a role to play that is irreplaceable and vital. We shouldn't settle for being mere spectators. Gradually, I came to see that there is a lot at stake in playing my part well, in being what the Church calls a "full, conscious and active" *participant* at Mass.

When a football team is losing and down to its last play, the quarterback will try to snatch victory from the jaws of defeat by throwing a "Hail Mary" pass. I imagine him in the huddle looking his receivers in the eyes and saying, "This is our last chance. I am counting on you." There is a lot at stake for these receivers. The outcome of the game is being placed in their hands. As dramatic as is that moment in a football game, it pales in comparison to what is at stake when we are "receivers" at Mass. What is placed in our hands is immeasurably more precious than a football, because it is not a *what*, but a *Who*: Jesus Christ. He is counting on you.

FOUR ENCOUNTERS WITH JESUS THAT WILL CHANGE YOUR LIFE

The Catholic Church teaches that Jesus Christ is present at Mass in four distinct ways: in the *community* gathered, in the *Word* proclaimed, in the *priest* who presides, and in the *Eucharist*. But He is not only present, He is active. In fact, the root meaning of the Latin word for "presence" is "to turn towards." Jesus Christ is present at Mass in these four ways, turned towards you, addressing you. Jesus Christ doesn't see a crowd at Mass. He sees you. He intends to come close to you, speak to you, live in you and change your life. As I became more aware of this, a sense of expectation and even drama grew in me. Will I recognize Jesus Christ turning toward me at Mass today? Once I knew that life-changing encounters with Jesus Christ awaited me at every Mass, I began to look and listen for Him with new eyes and ears. It was so much easier to pay attention when I realized what was at stake: missing out on meeting the living Lord, Jesus Christ.

You might be saying to yourself, "I have gone to Mass my whole life and have rarely, if ever, experienced a life changing encounter with Jesus." That's why I wrote this book. In it, I invite you to take a closer look at what you say and do during Mass. If you are like me and thousands of others who have discovered the message of this book, you will be amazed at what you've been missing.

Chapter by chapter, I accompany you from the time you pull into the church parking lot to the moment you walk out after the final blessing. If I do my job well, you will learn how to recognize and respond to Jesus Christ's drawing near you at Mass.

That's my goal: to help you see with new eyes what is so familiar to you, and hear with new ears what you've heard over and over at Mass so that you might respond well and be changed.

WHY THIS BOOK?

There are a number of books written with the goal of improving our understanding of the *ritual* of the Mass, by explaining its biblical roots, history or symbolism. Other books present theological insights or reflect on the correct way of celebrating Mass. Altogether, these books provide an invaluable service by deepening our appreciation for the mystery and majesty of the Mass.

But I have yet to find a book that examines the Mass, from beginning to end, as an event. That is what I do in this book. At Mass you are involved in a *ritual* that is an event. By looking at the Mass as an event, I focus on how it is a point of contact, communication and communion with Jesus Christ. I will show that Jesus Christ approaches you through the ritual in ways that will change your life. This approach does not negate the value of the Mass as a ritual. Rather, it shows how the ritual of the Mass is itself *a crucial event*.

THE GREATEST SHOW ON EARTH

At Mass, when we participate in the ritual Jesus Christ instituted at the Last Supper, we come into contact with an event greater than the "greatest show on earth." To be sure, the Mass is not a show, but during Mass, the greatest "showing up" on earth occurs. Why? Because Jesus Christ shows up at Mass in ways He does nowhere else. But He doesn't just show up. By His presence in the community, the Word, the priest and the Eucharist, He invites us to encounter events that are overwhelming in their majesty and power.

At Mass:

1. Jesus Christ includes you in His thanks and praise of God the Father, uniting Heaven and earth in one *Community* of thanksgiving and worship.

2. He communicates with you as *Word*, speaking the personal message you most need to hear at that moment.

3. He involves you in the crucial event where He is both *Priest* and Victim, called the Paschal Mystery (Jesus' Passion, death, Resurrection and Ascension).

4. He approaches you as Bread from Heaven, to be

consumed by you in the *Eucharist* in order to transform you into Himself.

This is what happens at every Mass. In this book, I focus on these four encounters with Jesus Christ being offered to you. Your entire life is going to be changed. If only your eyes are open to see what is really happening. If only you have the ears to hear. If only you'll stop being a *spectator*. It's time to get off the sidelines and into the game. It's time to be a *participant*.

You tell me. Is this boring?